101 Ways to Get Your Adult Children to Move Out

(AND MAKE THEM THINK IT WAS THEIR IDEA)

Rich Melheim

MAIN STREET BOOKS
DOUBLEDAY

New York London Toronto Sydney Auckland

A MAIN STREET BOOK
PUBLISHED BY DOUBLEDAY
a division of Bantam Doubleday Dell Publishing Group, Inc.
1540 Broadway, New York, New York 10036

MAIN STREET BOOKS, DOUBLEDAY, and the portrayal of a building
with a tree are trademarks of Doubleday,
a division of Bantam Doubleday Dell Publishing Group, Inc.

Library of Congress Cataloging-in-Publication Data

Melheim, Richard Alan.
101 ways to get your adult children to move out : (and make them
think it was their idea) / Rich Melheim. — 1st Doubleday ed.
p.   cm.
"A Main Street book."
1. Parenting—Humor. 2. Adult children—Humor.
PN6231.P2M45 1996
818'.5402—dc20   95-32761
                                         CIP

ISBN 0-385-48006-7
Copyright © 1993, 1994, 1996 by Rich Melheim
All Rights Reserved
Printed in the United States of America

1   3   5   7   9   10   8   6   4   2

First Main Street Books Edition: February 1996

To Emma and Duds, Jim and Bev,
and all other frustrated parents who
believe that the end justifies the means.

Contents

Where to Begin

1.
Start a toenail collection.

2.

Grow and braid your nose hairs.

3.
Have your gallstones made
into a brooch.

4.

As a conversation piece, keep your recently removed appendix in a jar of formaldehyde on top of the television.

5.

Tell them you can spit farther
than they can.

6.
Change the frequency on the
garage-door opener.

7.

Blow your nose without a hankie.

8.

Blow your nose with a hankie and then use it to clean their glasses.

9.

Recycle your toilet paper.

10.
Wallpaper their bedroom with
"My Little Pony."

11.

Join the Hell's Angels Auxiliary and
volunteer your children to chair the
"entertainment committee."

12.
Iron a hole in every sixth shirt.

13.
Practice the Mike Ditka method of public body-part readjustment.

14.

Leave your toupee on the coatrack
upon entering the house.

15.

Develop a rare psychotic disorder that compels you to stand on one foot and yell "Mel Torme lives" whenever they mention the word "money."

Weekly Subtle Hints

16.

Weekly, drop their checkbook
into the toilet.

17.

Weekly, call them by their older brother's name.

18.

Weekly, back their car into
the garage wall.

19.
Weekly, parcel-post a third of
their laundry to Toledo.

20.

Weekly, ask them the consistency of their "stool." If they tell you, respond, "Boy, those were the good old days."

21.

Break down in tears once a week lamenting the fact that almost all of your ancestors are dead.

22.

Weekly, wash their underwear, socks, and all of their white shirts in hot water with a red sweater.

23.

Use their computer each Saturday morning while eating a jelly roll, White-Out all your mistakes on the screen, and accidentally erase something marked "hard disk."

24.

Invite the local religious cult to hold its weekly sing-along in your living room during "Cheers" reruns.

Selective Recall

25.

If female, forget to wear a bra.
If male, start wearing one.

26.

Volunteer to rotate their tires and halfway through the process remember you had a golf date.

27.

Accidentally forget a honey, Tabasco, and sardine sandwich in their briefcase.

28.

Accidentally forget their clothes in
the wash for the weekend.

29.

Accidentally forget where you
put their car keys.

30.
Accidentally forget where you put their car.

31.

Forget to take out the garbage.

32.
Forget to buy groceries.

33.
Forget to flush the toilet.

34.

Forget to wear clothes around the house.

35.

Late in the evening, send them into the garage to find a wrench. Forget you sent them. Then go to the neighbors and call the police to report an intruder.

General Annoyances

36.
Give their little dog a punk haircut.

37.
Liberally apply the words "mod," "groovy," and "farm out" to your conversation.

38.

Recreate the horse head scene from *The Godfather* in their bed.

39.

Ask "Where are you going?" and
"When will you be home?"
whenever they leave the house.

40.

Dress as your favorite All-Star Wrestler
and surprise them with a body slam
from behind the door each
night after work.

41.

Regularly borrow their car, siphon the gas, smear Ben-Gay on the manifold, leave a piece of Limburger cheese in the glove box, and retune the stereo-selection buttons to Southern evangelist and polka stations.

42.

Replace all toothpaste with denture cream.

43.
Replace all the liquor in your cabinet with prune juice.

44.

As an antitheft precaution, wood-burn
their initials onto every CD in
their music collection.

Special Friends

45.

Invite their special friend for an elegant, romantic dinner and halfway through the meal remove and clean your dentures with a fork.

46.

Regularly call their special friend by a former special friend's first name.

47.

Blow up a few of those old baby-bath and bear-skin-rug snapshots of your child and surprise that special friend with a cutie-nudie photo night.

48.

Whenever their special friend rises from a chair, whip out a large can of disinfectant and quickly spray the seat.

49.

Give a washed pair of lacy underwear to their special friend, saying, "Here, I think these are yours." When they tell you they aren't, simply reply, "Oh, I am sooooo embarrassed. They must belong to . . . ," turning to your child, "what's that other one's name again?"

50.

Offer to show the video of your prostate surgery to their special friend.

51.
Offer to show the scar.

52.

Try some new recipes on their special friend—like their rare, expensive, exotic fish on tapioca and waffles.

Evening Classics and TV Touches

53.

Learn the fine art of watching ESPN, CNN, NBC, ABC, CBS, and two scrambled movie channels simultaneously while controlling the remote.

54.

Whenever a Democrat appears on TV, turn the mute button on and shout, "We wouldn't be in this mess today if Nixon were still in the White House!"

55.

Trade in your big-screen stereo TV for a twelve-inch black-and-white model.

56.

Ask them to tape "Hee Haw" reruns for you and edit out all the commercials.

57.
Lock your TV on the Weather Channel.

58.

Break down crying every night when a beer commercial comes on and bellow, "Zounds, child! Do you realize that none of this would be possible if free speech were not guaranteed by the Constitution?"

59.

Whenever Bosnia, the Ebola virus, or crime in American cities are mentioned on the nightly news, turn off the TV and grumble, "I don't know why everyone gets so riled up about a bunch of dead communists."

60.

Purchase a snoring tape and a huge
stereo amplifier, place the speaker
directly across the wall from their bed,
and at 3 A.M. nightly blow the
plaster off their wall.

61.

At the stroke of midnight each full moon, enter their room buck-naked with hunting knives, chanting, "Redrum, redrum" ("murder" backward).

62.

Sit at the bathroom window with a loaded shotgun each night to protect your family from alien body snatchers.

63.

Tweak their cheek whenever they head to bed, saying, "Oh, it's so nice to have you around the house, my little apple dumpling."

64.

Sneak into their room nightly and drool on their face, singing:

"I love you forever,
I'll like you for always . . ."

More Annoyances

65.

Go on a diet and in all seriousness tell them that they must gain a pound for every pound you lose so as not to upset the equilibrium of the universe.

66.

Whenever their private telephone rings,
answer with "My little pookey's
answering service."

67.
Sew plaid elbow patches on all of their good suits.

68.

Rent the guest room across the hall to a Neanderthal.

69.

Trade in the Lawn Monster X-KE 386, with bagger, mulcher, and built-in wet bar, for the push mower that grandpa used to use.

70.
Try to squeeze a little tofu into every meal.

71.

Plant 490 zucchini sprouts in
Tupperware containers in the bathtub.

72.

Invent nine friends with infectious illnesses and repeat at least twelve times a night, "I wonder if that's what I have?"

Borderline Raunch

73.

Learn how to break wind to the tune of "Old MacDonald."

74.

Store your belly-button lint in a
Noxzema jar in the kitchen.

75.
Grow penicillin in their underwear drawer.

76.

Replumb the bathroom so that every time you flush the toilet the water in the faucet turns just a tad yellow.

77.

Practice knocking flies out of the
air with boogers.

78.

Lace all their favorite recipes
with Ex-Lax.

79.

Learn how to blow bubbles with saliva.

80.

Record your "Greatest Belches of
All Time" and play them for
your children's guests.

81.

Subscribe to a "Learn Proctology at Home" correspondence course that requires a human guinea pig for lab work.

82.

Stuff the fridge with your favorite dead animal parts.

83.

Exhume Fido and perform an autopsy on the living room table to determine cause of death.

84.

Describe your dear old friend Inman Hershinbecker's bowel resection in detail during supper.

85.

Develop a neurosis about radon gas
and place five-day deodorant pads
soaked in kerosene around the house
to absorb the deadly gases.
(You read about it in *The Enquirer*.)

86.

From now until they move out,
nightly ask, "Did I ever tell you about
my dear old friend Inman
Hershinbecker's bowel resection?"

If All Else Fails . . .

87.

Give their name as a hot prospect to the Marines, the Jehovah's Witnesses, and Amway.

88.

Start telling knock-knock jokes.

89.

Call your child's superiors at work to tell them that your little genius should be paid what she/he is worth.

90.

Call the superiors back a day later and
ask if the salary has been adjusted yet, or
if you have to go higher up in the
company to get results.

91.
Ask to borrow money.

92.
Buy this book.

93.

Raise fly larvae on leftovers
in the fridge.

94.

Raise another batch of children.

95.
Raze your house and move.

96.

Raise llamas in the living room.

97.

Take them on a two-week bus tour to
the Corn Palace in Mitchell,
South Dakota.

98.
Start a beginners banjo, bagpipe,
and clarinet band.

99.

Join the NRA, subscribe to the *Mercenary Journal,* and place a live cluster bomb on the end table as a conversation piece.

100.

Talk often of your dear friend Tillie Bergine Smrzinski who never married and who, at seventy-four, still lives at home to care for her ninety-seven-year-old mother.

101.

If you have tried all of these methods
and still have nothing to show for it,
ask nine or ten family friends to say
to your child:

"You are becoming more and more like
your parents every day."

Then start sneezing the word "rent"
whenever they walk into the room.
That ought to do it.

Good luck!